D1633991

YOU'RE THE SPRING IN MY STEP

Summersdale Publishers Ltd
46 West Street
Chichester
West Sussex
PO19 1RP
UK

www.summersdale.com

Printed and bound in the Czech Republic

ISBN: 978-1-84953-517-5

Substantial discounts on bulk quantities of Summersdale books are available to corporations, professional associations and other organisations. For details contact Nicky Douglas by telephone: +44 (0) 1243 756902, fax: +44 (0) 1243 786300 or email: nicky@summersdale.com.

THIS IS DEDICATED TO RACHEL,
MY BEAUTIFUL FIANCÉE.

A LADY WHO I LOVE, ADORE AND WHO
HAS CHANGED MY LIFE BEYOND COMPARE.

A LADY WHOSE SMILE CAN BRIGHTEN
THE DARKEST DAY, AND LETS ME
KNOW HOW MUCH SHE LOVES ME.

RACHEL YOU'RE AMAZING,
I WILL ALWAYS LOVE YOU !

JIM

To:......................

From:...................

YOU'RE THE

WHISKERS

ON MY

KITTEN

YOU'RE THE
FRED
TO MY GINGER

YOU'RE THE

RUM

IN MY COKE

YOU'RE THE
ROLLER
TO MY
DISCO

YOU'RE THE BUBBLES TO MY BATH

YOU'RE THE
DUNGEONS
TO MY DRAGONS

YOU'RE THE ICING ON MY CAKE

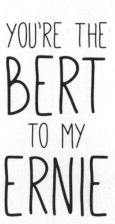

YOU'RE THE
BERT
TO MY
ERNIE

YOU'RE THE

NERD

TO MY

GEEK

YOU'RE THE TWIST TO MY SHOUT

You're the top

of my
pops

YOU'RE THE DISCS

FOR MY DESERT ISLAND

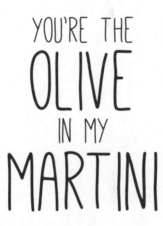

YOU'RE THE

MARIO

TO MY

LUIGI

YOU'RE THE LENNON TO MY McCARTNEY

YOU'RE THE PEANUT BUTTER TO MY JELLY

YOU'RE THE
SPRINKLES
ON MY WHIPPED
CREAM

YOU'RE THE
BLUE
TO MY SKY

YOU'RE THE WALL-E TO MY EVE

YOU'RE THE
BURGER
TO MY
FRIES

YOU'RE THE

AC

TO MY DC

you're the
romeo

to my

juliet

YOU'RE THE
GOLDEN
LEAVES
TO MY AUTUMN DAY

YOU'RE THE

CONTROLLER

TO MY

CONSOLE

YOU'RE THE
DOROTHY
TO MY TOTO

YOU'RE THE

WHIZZ

TO MY BANG

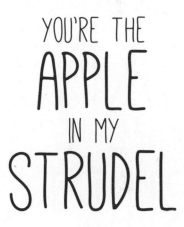

YOU'RE THE
APPLE
IN MY
STRUDEL

YOU'RE THE

SKINS

TO MY

SHIRTS

YOU'RE THE
BLOUSY
TO MY BUGSY

YOU'RE THE

SALT

TO MY PEPPER

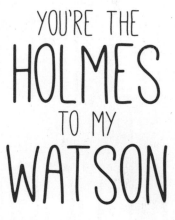

YOU'RE THE

HELIUM

TO MY

BALLOON

YOU'RE THE
REASON
TO MY WHY

you're the
tick

to my

tock

YOU'RE THE
BUTTER
ON MY CRUMPET

YOU'RE THE

SNOW

TO MY

CHRISTMAS DAY

YOU'RE THE
VINTAGE
TO MY
RETRO

YOU'RE THE
KERMIT
TO MY MISS PIGGY

YOU'RE THE
BOHEMIAN
TO MY RHAPSODY

YOU'RE THE
FINISHING LINE
TO MY
RACE

YOU'RE THE

PICNIC

TO MY

BLANKET

YOU'RE THE
UMBRELLA
IN MY COCKTAIL

YOU'RE THE
JELLY
TO MY CUSTARD

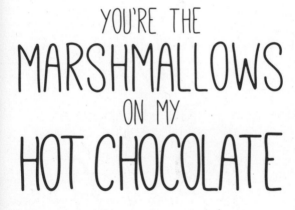

YOU'RE THE

OOH

TO MY

LA LA!

YOU'RE THE
CANDY
TO MY CRUSH

YOU'RE THE
THUNDER
TO MY LIGHTNING

you're the

beat

to my

heart

YOU'RE THE
ANSWER
TO MY
QUESTION

YOU'RE THE
RHYTHM
TO MY BLUES

YOU'RE THE
BONNIE
TO MY CLYDE

YOU'RE THE

CUCUMBER

IN MY

SANDWICH

YOU'RE THE
SIMON
TO MY GARFUNKEL.

YOU'RE THE

BACON

TO MY EGGS

YOU'RE THE

E

TO MY

MC²

YOU'RE THE
MORECAMBE
TO MY
WISE

YOU'RE THE
FIONA
TO MY SHREK

YOU'RE THE
NEEDLE
TO MY THREAD

YOU'RE THE
MEANING
TO MY
QUEST

you're the
nod

to my

wink

YOU'RE THE
BEAT
TO MY
DRUM

YOU'RE THE
FEATHER
IN MY CAP

YOU'RE THE
SAMWISE
TO MY FRODO

YOU'RE THE

YIN

TO MY

YANG

YOU'RE THE

HOME

TO MY AWAY

YOU'RE THE SPOONFUL OF SUGAR TO MY MEDICINE

YOU'RE THE

T'AI

TO MY

CHI

♥

YOU'RE THE
POP
TO MY
CORN

♥

YOU'RE THE
KNIGHT
TO MY STEED

YOU'RE THE FLAME TO MY CANDLE

you're the

wowie

to my

zowie

YOU'RE THE
MANI-PEDI
TO MY
SPA DAY

YOU'RE THE BUBBLE TO MY SQUEAK

YOU'RE THE
BATMAN
TO MY ROBIN

YOU'RE THE

FLIP

TO MY

FLOP

YOU'RE THE
PAGES
TO MY
BOOK

YOU'RE THE CHERRY ON MY SUNDAE

YOU'RE THE
TURBO
TO MY BOOSTER

YOU'RE THE
POT O' GOLD
TO MY
RAINBOW

YOU'RE THE

CARPE

TO MY

DIEM

YOU'RE THE

NOTES

TO MY MUSIC

YOU'RE THE
MULDER
TO MY SCULLY

YOU'RE THE
NEEDLE
IN MY
HAYSTACK

you're the
hip

to my

hop

♥

——— YOU'RE THE ———

KETCHUP

TO MY

CHIPS

♥

YOU'RE THE
LIFE
& SOUL
TO MY PARTY

YOU'RE THE
SPICE
IN MY LIFE

YOU'RE THE

ORANGES

TO MY

LEMONS

YOU'RE THE

TINTIN

TO MY

SNOWY

YOU'RE THE

STARS

TO MY STRIPES

YOU'RE THE
PONGO
TO MY PERDITA

YOU'RE THE
CREAM
IN MY
OREO

♥

YOU'RE THE
PIGLET
TO MY
POOH

♥

YOU'RE THE BROLLY TO MY RAINY DAY

YOU'RE THE PESTO ON MY PASTA

YOU'RE THE
FORTUNE
IN MY
COOKIE

you're the

lol

to my

omg

YOU'RE THE
ZIG
TO MY
ZAG

YOU'RE THE

CTRL

TO MY ALT-DEL

YOU'RE THE

TOM

TO MY COLLINS

YOU'RE THE

CRESTS

ON MY

WAVES

YOU'RE THE

RABBIT

IN MY

HAT

YOU'RE THE

VIVE

TO MY DIFFÉRENCE

YOU'RE THE DIAMOND TO MY ROUGH

YOU'RE THE

9

TO MY

5

YOU'RE THE

Y

TO MY

MCA

YOU'RE THE
BUTTERED
SOLDIERS
TO MY BOILED EGG

YOU'RE THE
STARS
IN MY SKY

YOU'RE THE
BUZZ
TO MY
WOODY

you're the
bucket

to my

spade

YOU'RE THE
TOP HAT
TO MY
TAILS

YOU'RE THE
SAUCER
TO MY CUP

YOU'RE THE
KNIGHTS
TO MY ROUND TABLE

YOU'RE THE
BANG
TO MY
BUCK

YOU'RE THE

BEANS

ON MY

TOAST

YOU'RE THE
CHEESE
TO MY PINEAPPLE

YOU'RE THE

SINE

TO MY COSINE

YOU'RE THE
R2D2
TO MY
C-3PO

YOU'RE THE

RADIO

TO MY

GA GA

YOU'RE THE
RAMA LAMA
TO MY DING DONG

YOU'RE THE CHOCOLATE IN MY MOCHA

YOU'RE THE

HELTER

TO MY

SKELTER

you're the

fred

to my

wilma

YOU'RE THE
CAGNEY
TO MY LACEY

YOU'RE THE
FRUIT
IN MY SANGRIA

YOU'RE THE
HARRY
TO MY
RON

YOU'RE THE

SKIP

TO MY

HEARTBEAT

YOU'RE THE
ICE CREAM
TO MY SUNNY DAY

YOU'RE THE BLING IN MY RING

YOU'RE THE
MOON
TO MY
STARS

YOU'RE THE
KEY
TO MY HEART

YOU'RE THE RAZZLE TO MY DAZZLE

YOU'RE THE
HAPPY ENDING
TO MY
STORY

you're the
spring

in my

step

IF YOU'RE INTERESTED IN FINDING OUT MORE ABOUT OUR BOOKS, FIND US ON FACEBOOK AT **summersdale publishers** AND FOLLOW US ON TWITTER AT **@summersdale**.